MAJOR DISASTERS

HURRICANE KATRINA

BY TRUDY BECKER

WWW.APEXEDITIONS.COM

Copyright © 2024 by Apex Editions, Mendota Heights, MN 55120. All rights reserved. No part of this book may be reproduced or utilized in any form or by any means without written permission from the publisher.

Apex is distributed by North Star Editions:
sales@northstareditions.com | 888-417-0195

Produced for Apex by Red Line Editorial.

Photographs ©: David J. Phillip/AP Images, cover; Eric Gay/AP Images, 1, 14, 25; Dave Martin/AP Images, 4–5, 8–9; Haraz N. Ghanbari and Gerald Herbert/AP Images, 6; Haraz N. Ghanbari/AP Images, 10–11; Shutterstock Images, 12–13, 16–17, 18–19, 20–21, 22–23, 26, 29; Gerald Herbert/AP Images, 24

Library of Congress Control Number: 2023910168

ISBN
978-1-63738-758-0 (hardcover)
978-1-63738-801-3 (paperback)
978-1-63738-884-6 (ebook pdf)
978-1-63738-844-0 (hosted ebook)

Printed in the United States of America
Mankato, MN
012024

NOTE TO PARENTS AND EDUCATORS

Apex books are designed to build literacy skills in striving readers. Exciting, high-interest content attracts and holds readers' attention. The text is carefully leveled to allow students to achieve success quickly. Additional features, such as bolded glossary words for difficult terms, help build comprehension.

CHAPTER 1
WALLS OF WATER ... 4

CHAPTER 2
HOW IT HAPPENED ... 10

CHAPTER 3
MASSIVE DAMAGE ... 16

CHAPTER 4
RESPONSE ... 22

COMPREHENSION QUESTIONS • 28
GLOSSARY • 30
TO LEARN MORE • 31
ABOUT THE AUTHOR • 31
INDEX • 32

CHAPTER 1

WALLS OF WATER

Rain pours down, and strong winds whip. **Hurricane** Katrina blows walls of water toward New Orleans, Louisiana.

4

Rushing water filled many streets in US cities during Hurricane Katrina.

Soon, huge waves rise. The water crashes into the city's **levees**. The levees aren't strong enough. They break. More water rushes into the city.

LEAVING THE AREA

The mayor of New Orleans ordered people to **evacuate**. But many people stayed. Some didn't want to leave. Others couldn't. They lacked cars or money to travel.

◀ Levees hold back water. When they collapse, nearby areas can flood.

People scramble to find safety. They climb to the roofs of houses. When the storm stops, rescuers come. They use boats and helicopters to look for survivors.

FAST FACT
A few days after the storm, around 80 percent of New Orleans was underwater.

In some places, more than 10 feet (3 m) of water covered the ground.

CHAPTER 2

How It Happened

Katrina was a huge storm that took place in August 2005. It began forming over the Atlantic Ocean. Wind caused thunderstorms to swirl. They became a **tropical storm**.

Katrina damaged large areas along the US coast.

The storm's winds grew faster and stronger. Soon, it became a hurricane. This large storm moved toward the Gulf of Mexico.

FAST FACT

Hurricane Katrina's winds reached 175 miles per hour (282 km/h).

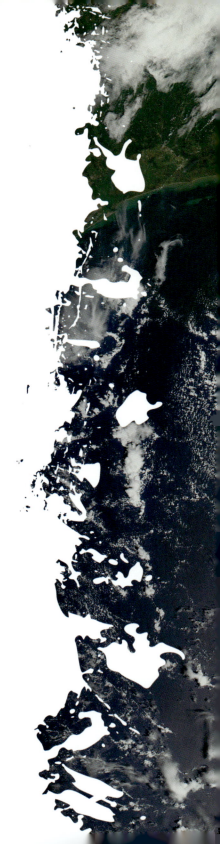

Hurricane Katrina reached the US coast on August 29, 2005.

When the storm hit land, it was more than 400 miles (644 km) wide. It brought heavy rain. It also caused a massive **storm surge**.

BIG IMPACT

Katrina hit several US states. These included Alabama, Florida, Louisiana, and Mississippi. The worst damage was in New Orleans. Much of this city is below sea level. So, it's at big risk for floods.

◀ A hurricane's rushing water can sweep away everything in its path.

CHAPTER 3

MASSIVE DAMAGE

Hurricane Katrina caused huge amounts of damage. Strong winds knocked down trees and power lines.

Hurricane Katrina's wind and water flung and smashed boats, cars, and houses.

The rain and storm surge caused dangerous flooding. Rising water covered roads. Some people became **stranded**. Others drowned. Hundreds of thousands lost their homes.

Hurricane Katrina smashed more than 40 bridges near the coast.

FAST FACT

Katrina was one of the deadliest hurricanes in US history. More than 1,800 people died.

When the water finally lowered, many buildings had fallen apart.

Many areas stayed flooded for weeks. Thousands of people lacked electricity. Food and water were hard to get.

THE LOWER NINTH WARD

The Lower Ninth Ward is a neighborhood in New Orleans. Damage there was especially bad. Deep water covered most of it. Streets, homes, and stores were destroyed.

CHAPTER 4

RESPONSE

After the storm, many groups sent help and supplies. They also tried to find places for people to stay. In many cases, this response was too slow. People died while waiting for help.

US leaders sent members of the military to help after the storm. But few arrived quickly.

Governments studied what went wrong. They tried to make better plans. They also built new levees and **seawalls**. That way, people would stay safer in future storms.

New Orleans replaced its broken levees with stronger ones.

The Superdome is a sports stadium in New Orleans. People gathered there during and after the hurricane.

THE SUPERDOME

During Katrina, the Superdome was used as a **shelter**. It quickly became too crowded. Supplies of food and water ran low. The storm also broke part of the roof.

People worked to rebuild damaged areas. Many places took years to recover. Others never did. The disaster had many lasting impacts.

FAST FACT
Biloxi, Alabama, lost almost one-fifth of its buildings in the storm. Many still hadn't been fixed in 2020.

◀ In the 2020s, some of the hardest-hit areas along the Gulf Coast still weren't rebuilt.

COMPREHENSION QUESTIONS

Write your answers on a separate piece of paper.

1. Write a few sentences describing some of the damage Hurricane Katrina caused.

2. Which way of predicting or preparing for a hurricane do you think is most important?

3. Which place had the worst damage from Hurricane Katrina?

    A. Alabama
    B. Mississippi
    C. New Orleans

4. Why would being below sea level increase a place's risk of floods?

    A. Ocean waves cannot cause floods.
    B. Even a small rise in water could cover the ground.
    C. Places that are below sea level get less rain.

5. What does **rescuers** mean in this book?

*When the storm stops, **rescuers** come. They use boats and helicopters to look for survivors.*

    A. people who stay far away from danger
    B. people who try to help or save others
    C. people who harm others on purpose

6. What does **recover** mean in this book?

*People worked to rebuild damaged areas. Many places took years to **recover**. Others never did.*

    A. be damaged by a disaster
    B. stay exactly the same as always
    C. return to how things were before

Answer key on page 32.

GLOSSARY

evacuate
To leave an area because it is not safe.

hurricane
A storm with spinning winds that are at least 74 miles per hour (119 km/h).

levees
Walls built to block rising water and stop floods.

seawalls
Walls built on coasts to protect the land from ocean waves.

shelter
A place that keeps people safe from danger.

storm surge
A rush of ocean water that storm winds blow toward the shore.

stranded
Stuck in a place and not able to leave.

tropical storm
A storm with spinning winds that go more than 39 miles per hour (63 km/h) but less than 74 miles per hour (119 km/h).

BOOKS

Dykstra, Mary. *Climate Change and Extreme Storms*. Minneapolis: Lerner Publications, 2019.

Rathburn, Betsy. *Hurricanes*. Minneapolis: Bellwether Media, 2020.

Rossiter, Brienna. *Hurricanes*. Mendota Heights, MN: Apex Editions, 2023.

ONLINE RESOURCES

Visit **www.apexeditions.com** to find links and resources related to this title.

ABOUT THE AUTHOR

Trudy Becker lives in Minneapolis, Minnesota. She likes exploring new places and loves anything involving books.

INDEX

A
Alabama, 15, 27
Atlantic Ocean, 10

E
evacuate, 7

F
flooding, 15, 18, 20

G
Gulf of Mexico, 12

L
levees, 7, 24
Lower Ninth Ward, 21

N
New Orleans, Louisiana, 4, 7–8, 15, 21

R
rain, 4, 15, 18

S
seawalls, 24
storm surge, 15, 18
Superdome, 25

T
tropical storm, 10

W
water, 4, 7–8, 18, 20–21, 25
winds, 4, 10, 12, 16

ANSWER KEY:
1. Answers will vary; 2. Answers will vary; 3. C; 4. B; 5. B; 6. C